burgers

burgers

Louise Pickford photography by Martin Brigdale

RYLAND
PETERS
& SMALL
LONDON NEW YORK

Senior Designer Steve Painter
Commissioning Editor
   Elsa Petersen-Schepelern
Editor Susan Stuck
Production Gavin Bradshaw
Art Director Anne-Marie Bulat
Editorial Director Julia Charles
Publishing Director Alison Starling

Food Stylist Bridget Sargeson
Stylist Helen Trent

First published in the USA in 2006
by Ryland Peters & Small, Inc.
519 Broadway, 5th Floor
New York, NY 10012
www.rylandpeters.com

10 9 8 7 6 5 4 3 2 1

Text © Louise Pickford 2006
Design and photographs
© Ryland Peters & Small 2006

Printed in China

Library of Congress Cataloging-in-
Publication Data

Pickford, Louise.
  Burgers / Louise Pickford ; photography
by Martin Brigdale.
     p. cm.
  Includes index.
  ISBN-13: 978-1-84597-138-0
  ISBN-10: 1-84597-138-8
  1. Cookery (Beef) I. Title.
  TX749.P53 2006
  641.6'62--dc22

                                    2005018970

Notes
• All spoon measurements are level unless
otherwise specified.
• All eggs are extra-large. Uncooked or partially
cooked eggs should not be served to the very
young, the very old, those with compromised
immune systems, or to pregnant women.
• To sterilize jam jars, wash them in hot, soapy
water and rinse in boiling water. Put in a large
saucepan and cover with hot water. With the lid
on, bring the water to a boil and continue boiling
for 15 minutes. Turn off the heat, then leave the
jars in the hot water until just before they are to
be filled. Invert the jars onto a clean cloth to dry.
Sterilize the lids for 5 minutes, by boiling, or
according to the manufacturer's instructions. The
jars should be filled and sealed while still hot.

contents

introduction

The burger is perhaps the most famous sandwich on the planet. It has a long history that can be traced from Mongolia to Russia, Germany, and the US. German immigrants arriving in New York in the late 18th century introduced grilled ground beef flavored with onion and spices, known as Hamburg steak. In New York City, Delmonico's restaurant is documented as serving hamburger steaks in the 1830s for a mere 10 cents. In the last 50 years, it has become the most popular takeout food of all, but its very popularity is probably what has made us forget how much better a homemade version can be.

What makes this sandwich so universally appealing? A good homemade burger is substantial, smoky from the grill, tangy with ketchup or mustard, comforting, and portable. At home, you can make burgers ranging from the classic beef patty to versions using lamb, pork, chicken, and turkey as well as vegetarian burgers made with chickpeas, beans, vegetables, tofu, and nuts, and flavored with a variety of herbs and spices.

What remains constant is that a burger is a simple combination of a few ingredients, easy to prepare and quick to cook. A good burger is a sumptuous feast, an explosion of flavors—a real treat for the taste buds. It's no surprise that this action-packed sandwich has become one of the world's most loved foods.

making, shaping, and cooking burgers

Using meat and poultry

Beef, pork, lamb, chicken, and turkey all make great burgers. Buy steaks or whole cuts and either coarsely grind your own meat or get the butcher to do it for you. You can use a food processor, but do not over-process the meat or it can be spongy and tough. If you buy ready-ground meat, buy a premium quality product.

The ideal cuts for a burger needn't be expensive. Choose meat with at least 20 percent fat—it keeps meat moist but also drains off as it cooks. Shank or chuck steak are good for beef; shoulder or leg for lamb and pork. Use skinless breast meat for chicken and turkey. Let the meat rest after it has been worked—this helps the protein relax, giving you a more tender burger when cooked.

Shaping burgers

I recommend thick burgers (large or small) so that the outside will be lightly charred allowing the center to stay moist. Wet your hands before shaping to stop the mixture sticking to you. Shape the mixture into a ball, then flatten into a patty.

Beef and lamb burgers can be cooked rare, but pork and chicken must be cooked through. Large patties take 5 to 6 minutes on each side, while smaller ones take 3 to 4 minutes each side. To test that a patty is cooked through, insert a metal skewer briefly into the center, then pull it out—the point should feel hot to touch, not cold.

Cooking methods

Burgers can be broiled, sautéed, or best of all grilled. There is nothing more delicious than the flavor of flame-grilled meat. That lovely smoky, lightly charred flavor coupled with a tender, moist center. If using coals make sure all flames have died down and are ashen before cooking the burgers. Preheat a gas grill for 10 to 15 minutes to make sure it is hot enough.

A stovetop grill pan is the next best cooking method. Preheat the pan for 5 minutes before cooking the patty. Sautéing is a good alternative for more delicate patties, such as vegetarian burgers or those coated with bread crumbs. Pour a shallow layer of oil into a heavy skillet and heat until almost smoking before adding the patty. Lower the heat to medium and continue to cook.

Use a broiler as a final option. Again, preheat the broiler until hot and cook the patties about 2 inches below the heat source, placing them on a rack over a foil-lined broiler pan.

meat

For a burger to be truly "all American," it must be served in a bun with lettuce, tomato, yellow mustard, and dill pickles with french fries on the side.

classic all-american hamburger

1½ lb. ground chuck

1 onion, finely chopped

1 teaspoon Worcestershire sauce

4 sesame seed buns, cut in half

2 tablespoons yellow mustard, plus extra to serve

about 1 cup shredded lettuce

2 tomatoes, sliced

2 dill pickles, sliced

sea salt and freshly ground black pepper

olive oil, for brushing

French Fries, to serve (page 51)

Serves 4

Put the beef, onion, Worcestershire sauce, and some salt and pepper in a bowl and work together with your hands until evenly mixed. Divide the mixture into 4 portions and shape into patties. Cover and chill for 30 minutes.

Brush the patties lightly with oil and grill or broil for 4 to 5 minutes on each side until lightly charred on the outside and just cooked through inside.

Meanwhile, toast the buns and spread one half of each with mustard. Add the shredded lettuce, patties, tomato slices, and dill pickles, squeeze over a little extra mustard, and add the bun tops. Serve at once with french fries.

This version of a cheeseburger is made using a good quality cheese cut into slices rather than the processed cheese often used. You can vary the cheese—for something a little different, try Camembert or crumbled Roquefort.

cheeseburger

1½ lb. ground chuck

1 onion, finely chopped

1 garlic clove, crushed

2 teaspoons chopped fresh thyme

4 burger buns, cut in half

4 tablespoons Mayonnaise (page 52)

4 large leaves of butterhead lettuce

4 oz. Cheddar cheese, sliced

2 tomatoes, sliced

½ red onion, thinly sliced

sea salt and freshly ground black pepper

olive oil, for brushing

Serves 4

Put the beef, onion, garlic, thyme, and some salt and pepper in a bowl and work together with your hands until evenly mixed and slightly sticky. Divide the mixture into 4 portions and shape into patties. Cover and chill for 30 minutes.

Brush the patties lightly with oil and grill or broil for 5 minutes on each side until lightly charred and cooked through. Top the burgers with the cheese slices and set under a hot broiler for 30 seconds until the cheese has melted. Keep them warm.

Toast the buns, then spread the base and tops with mayonnaise. Add the lettuce leaves, cheese-topped patties, and tomato and onion slices. Add the bun tops and serve hot.

A substantial multi-layered burger makes the perfect brunch meal. You could also add broiled mushrooms if you liked.

triple whammy breakfast burger

1½ lb. Prime ground beef

1 onion, finely chopped

1 tablespoon wholegrain mustard

4 English muffins, cut in half

4 slices of lean smoked bacon

4 plum tomatoes, sliced

4 eggs

sea salt and freshly ground black pepper

olive oil, for brushing

peanut or safflower oil, for sautéing

Homemade Tomato Ketchup, to serve (page 55)

Serves 4

Put the beef, onion, mustard, and some salt and pepper in a bowl and work together with your hands until evenly mixed and slightly sticky. Divide into 4 portions and shape into patties. Cover and chill for 30 minutes.

Brush the patties lightly with olive oil and grill or pan-grill for 4 to 5 minutes on each side until lightly charred and cooked through. Keep them warm.

Meanwhile, heat a skillet until hot and dry-fry the bacon for 2 to 3 minutes on each side until crisp. Keep warm with the burgers. Add the tomatoes to the skillet and sauté for 2 minutes on each side and keep them warm. Heat a shallow layer of peanut or safflower oil in the skillet, add the eggs, and cook for 2 to 3 minutes until cooked to your liking.

Toast the muffins. Put the tomato slices on the bases, followed by the patties, bacon, and fried egg. Spoon over some ketchup and add the muffin tops. Serve hot.

Kids love burgers and these are served as sausage shapes in a hot dog roll. Alternatively, shape as the more traditional patties and serve in small toasted buns. You can add some shredded lettuce and tomatoes to the burger for a healthier option.

"sausage" burgers for kids

1 lb. Prime ground beef

2 teaspoons onion powder

2 tablespoons Homemade Tomato Ketchup (page 55), plus extra for serving

2 tablespoons chopped fresh flat-leaf parsley

8 hot dog rolls

¼ cup grated Cheddar cheese

sea salt and freshly ground black pepper

olive oil, for brushing

Serves 4

Put the beef, onion powder, tomato ketchup, parsley, and a little salt and pepper in a bowl and work together with your hands until evenly mixed and slightly sticky. Divide into 4 portions and mold into long thin sausage shapes. Cover and chill for 30 minutes.

Brush the "sausage" burgers lightly with oil and cook on a preheated ridged stovetop grill pan (or heavy skillet) for 7 to 8 minutes, turning frequently until cooked through.

Split the rolls horizontally without cutting all the way through. Put a "sausage" in each one and sprinkle with some grated cheese and tomato ketchup. Serve hot.

The flavors of Texas and Mexico combine well in this tangy burger. For those who really like it hot, try the Caribbean version with the fiery chile sauce.

tex-mex burger
with chile relish

1½ lb. ground chuck

1 small red onion, finely chopped

1 garlic clove, crushed

2 teaspoons dried Mexican oregano

1½ teaspoons ground cumin

2 burger buns, cut in half

1 cup shredded iceberg lettuce

¼ cup grated Cheddar cheese

sea salt and freshly ground black pepper

olive oil, for brushing

Chile relish

1 lb. tomatoes, coarsely chopped

1 red onion, coarsely chopped

2 garlic cloves, crushed

2–4 jalapeño chiles, coarsely chopped

2 tablespoons Worcestershire sauce

1 cup soft brown sugar

⅔ cup red wine vinegar

2 teaspoons sea salt

Serves 4

To make the chile relish, put the tomatoes, onion, garlic, and chiles in a food processor and blend until smooth. Transfer the mixture to a saucepan, add the Worcestershire sauce, sugar, vinegar, and 2 teaspoons salt. Bring to a boil and simmer gently for 30 to 40 minutes until the sauce has thickened. Let cool completely and refrigerate until required.

Put the beef, onion, garlic, oregano, cumin, and some salt and pepper in a bowl and work together with your hands until evenly mixed and sticky. Divide into 4 portions and shape into patties. Cover and chill for 30 minutes.

Brush the patties lightly with oil and grill or broil for 4 to 5 minutes on each side until cooked through. Keep them warm.

Lightly toast the buns. Top each half with shredded lettuce, a patty, some grated cheese, and chile relish. Serve hot.

Variation Caribbean Chile Burger

Make the chile relish as above, replacing the jalapeño chiles with 1 Scotch bonnet or habanero chile, seeded and chopped. When assembling the burger, add a layer of sliced avocado to help temper the fire of the extra hot chile sauce (use disposable latex gloves when handling Scotch bonnet or habanero chiles).

Pork adds extra flavor and fat to these beef patties, keeping them beautifully moist as they cook.

1½ lb. chuck steak, coarsely chopped

4 oz. pork from the arm or blade, coarsely chopped

1 cup fresh white bread crumbs

1 egg, lightly beaten

a few drops of Tabasco sauce

1 onion, thinly sliced into rings

⅔ cup milk

2 tablespoons all-purpose flour, seasoned with salt and pepper

4 hero rolls

a handful of baby spinach leaves

2 tomatoes, sliced

4 tablespoons Hot and Smoky Barbecue Sauce (page 55)

sea salt and freshly ground black pepper

olive oil, for brushing

peanut or safflower oil, for deep-frying

an electric deep-fryer (optional)

Serves 4

grilled beef burger
with crispy onion rings

Put the beef and pork in a food processor and blend briefly until just ground. Transfer to a bowl and add the bread crumbs, egg, Tabasco, salt, and pepper and work together with your hands until evenly mixed and slightly sticky. Cover and chill for 30 minutes, then shape into 8 small patties.

Meanwhile, soak the onion rings in the milk for 30 minutes.

Brush the patties lightly with olive oil and grill or broil for 3 minutes on each side until lightly charred and cooked through. Keep them warm.

Meanwhile, drain the soaked onion rings and dust with seasoned flour. Heat 2 inches peanut or safflower oil in a deep, heavy saucepan until it reaches 350°F on a deep-fry thermometer. Add the onion rings, in batches, and deep-fry for 2 to 3 minutes until crisp and golden. Drain on paper towels. Alternatively, use an electric deep-fryer and follow the manufacturer's instructions.

Slice the rolls almost in half, open out, and toast lightly on both sides. Fill the rolls with spinach leaves, tomato slices, 2 patties, barbecue sauce, and serve topped with the crispy onion rings.

Although not strictly speaking a burger, this is the ultimate beef sandwich.

steak sandwich
with shoestring potatoes

¼ cup olive oil, plus extra for brushing

2 onions, thinly sliced

1½ lb. sirloin steaks

4 small baguettes, cut in half lengthwise

½ cup Mustard Mayonnaise (page 52)

4 oz. watercress leaves

sea salt and freshly ground black pepper

1 recipe Shoestring Potatoes, to serve (page 51)

Serves 4

Heat the oil in a skillet, add the onions, season with salt and pepper, and sauté over medium heat for 20 to 25 minutes until golden and caramelized. Keep them warm.

Brush the steaks with oil and season liberally with salt and pepper. Preheat a heavy skillet until hot and sauté the steaks for 3 minutes on each side for rare, 4 minutes for medium, and 5 minutes for well done. Let rest for 5 minutes, then slice thickly.

Meanwhile, lightly toast the baguettes and spread the insides liberally with mustard mayonnaise. Fill with watercress leaves, the sliced beef and all the juices, and top with the onions. Serve hot with shoestring potatoes.

The smoky taste of bacon adds great flavor to these patties, which are equally good made from ground chicken for a change. Use a meat grinder or food processor to grind the meat and bacon.

bacon burger
with creamy coleslaw

1¼ lb. Prime ground beef

4 oz. (about 4 slices) bacon, ground

1 onion, finely chopped

1 garlic clove, crushed

1 tablespoon chopped fresh sage leaves

1 egg yolk

1 tablespoon wholegrain mustard

4 poppy seed rolls, cut in half

4 iceberg lettuce leaves

2 tomatoes, sliced

½ recipe Sour Cream Coleslaw (page 56)

sea salt and freshly ground black pepper

olive oil, for brushing

Serves 4

Put the beef, bacon, onion, garlic, sage, egg yolk, mustard, and some salt and pepper in a bowl and work together with your hands to form a slightly sticky mixture. Divide into 4 portions and shape into patties. Cover and chill for 30 minutes.

Brush the patties lightly with oil and grill or broil for 5 minutes on each side until cooked through. Keep warm.

Toast the rolls and fill them with lettuce leaves, tomato slices, the patties, and coleslaw. Serve hot.

Lamb makes a lovely alternative to beef. You could use meat from the shoulder or leg, and grind or process it coarsely yourself.

mediterranean lamb burger

1½ lb. ground lamb

1 small onion, finely chopped

1 tablespoon chopped fresh mint leaves

2 teaspoon dried oregano

6 anchovies in oil, drained and chopped

4 plum tomatoes, cut in half

4 slices of ciabatta or focaccia

1 garlic clove, left whole

about 6 oz. mozzarella cheese ball, sliced

a handful of fresh basil leaves

sea salt and freshly ground black pepper

olive oil, for brushing and sprinkling

Arugula, Radicchio, and Crisp Bacon Salad, to serve (page 59)

Serves 4

Put the lamb, onion, mint, oregano, anchovies, and some salt and pepper in a bowl and work together with your hands until evenly mixed. Divide into 4 portions and shape into patties. Cover and chill for 30 minutes.

Brush the patties lightly with oil and grill or broil for 4 to 5 minutes on each side until cooked through. Keep them warm.

Meanwhile, arrange the tomatoes halves on a broiler pan, season with salt and pepper, and drizzle with a little oil. Cook under a preheated hot broiler for 2 to 3 minutes until softened.

Grill or broil the ciabatta or focaccia slices and rub all over with the whole garlic and drizzle with oil. Transfer to serving plates and top each slice with a patty, a slice of mozzarella, a broiled tomato, and some basil leaves. Serve at once with the arugula, radicchio, and crisp bacon salad.

1½ lb. ground pork

2 garlic cloves, crushed

1 teaspoon grated fresh ginger

2 tablespoons chopped
fresh cilantro

2 tablespoons cornstarch

1 egg, lightly beaten

4 hero rolls

a handful of fresh herbs,
such as Thai or plain basil,
cilantro, and mint leaves

sea salt and freshly
ground black pepper

peanut or safflower oil,
for brushing

Satay sauce

¼ cup chunky peanut butter

2 tablespoons coconut cream

2 tablespoons freshly squeezed
lime juice

1 tablespoons sweet chile sauce,
plus extra for serving

2 teaspoons light soy sauce

1 teaspoon soft brown sugar

12 bamboo skewers, soaked in
cold water for 30 minutes

Serves 4

This burger is inspired by some of the wonderful pork skewers they serve in Thai restaurants, with their great use of fresh herbs and satay sauce.

spiced pork burger
with satay sauce

Put the pork, garlic, ginger, cilantro, cornstarch, egg, and some salt and pepper in a bowl and work together with your hands until well mixed. Divide into 12 portions and shape into small logs. Cover and chill for 30 minutes.

Meanwhile, to make the satay sauce, put the peanut butter, coconut cream, lime juice, chile sauce, soy sauce, and brown sugar in a small saucepan and heat gently, stirring until mixed. Simmer gently for 1 to 2 minutes until thickened. Set aside to cool.

Thread the patties onto the soaked skewers and brush with oil. Grill or broil for 6 to 8 minutes, turning frequently until charred on the outside and cooked through. Keep them warm.

To serve, split the rolls down the middle, open out, and fill with herbs. Remove the skewers from the pork patties and add the patties to the rolls along with some satay sauce and sweet chile sauce. Serve hot.

chicken and poultry

Chicken makes a lighter burger than meat but is no less delicious. Make sure you don't overwork the mixture as you process it—use the pulse button and blend briefly, checking the mixture each time before processing again. Use wet hands to shape the patties.

1½ lb. skinless boneless chicken breasts, ground

1 tablespoon milk

1 small onion, finely chopped

2 garlic cloves, crushed

4 sesame seed buns, cut in half

4 tablespoons Herb Mayonnaise (page 52), plus extra to serve

a handful of baby spinach leaves

2 tomatoes, sliced

sea salt and freshly ground black pepper

olive oil, for brushing

Serves 4

chicken burger
with herb mayonnaise

Put the chicken, milk, onion, garlic, and some salt and pepper in a food processor and pulse until smooth. Transfer the mixture to a bowl, cover, and chill for 30 minutes. Divide the mixture into 4 portions and shape into patties.

Brush the patties lightly with olive oil and grill or broil for 5 to 6 minutes on each side until cooked through. Test one by inserting a metal skewer into the center—it should feel hot to the touch when the patty is cooked. Keep them warm.

Lightly toast the buns and spread the top halves with some herb mayonnaise. Fill the buns with spinach leaves, patties, and tomato slices, and serve with extra herb mayonnaise.

1½ lb. skinless boneless chicken breasts, coarsely chopped

1 cup fresh white bread crumbs

freshly grated zest of 1 unwaxed lime

2 teaspoons Creole seasoning

2–3 tablespoons all-purpose flour, seasoned with salt and pepper

2 eggs, lightly beaten

¾ cup medium cornmeal

2 burger buns, cut in half

1 cup shredded romaine lettuce

4 tablespoons Mayonnaise (page 52)

sea salt and freshly ground black pepper

peanut or safflower oil, for sautéing

Hot and Smoky Barbecue Sauce, to serve (page 55) (optional)

Creole salsa

2 tomatoes, chopped

½ red onion, finely chopped

1 jalapeño chile, finely chopped

freshly squeezed juice of 1 lime

1 tablespoon chopped fresh cilantro

Serves 4

Creole cooking is mainly associated with the Mississippi Delta, where traditions of French, Spanish, and African foods combine. Readymade spice mixes are available from supermarkets and specialty food stores.

creole spiced chicken burger

Put the chicken and 1 tablespoon water in a food processor and pulse until just ground. Add the bread crumbs, lime zest, Creole seasoning, and some salt and pepper and pulse until smooth. Transfer the mixture to a bowl, cover and chill for 30 minutes.

Divide the mixture into 8 portions and shape into patties. Dust the patties lightly with seasoned flour and dip them first into the egg, then the cornmeal to coat thoroughly.

Heat a shallow layer of oil in a nonstick skillet, add the patties, and sauté for 3 minutes on each side until golden and cooked through. Drain on paper towels and keep them warm.

Meanwhile, to make the salsa, put the tomatoes, onion, chile, lime juice, and cilantro in a bowl and season to taste with salt and pepper. Mix well and set aside until required.

Lightly toast the buns, top each half with shredded lettuce, 2 burger patties, some mayonnaise, the salsa, and some barbecue sauce, if using. Serve hot.

The Caesar salad is as much an American icon as the burger and here the two combine perfectly in a great sourdough sandwich. You can add a poached egg to the filling, if you like.

4 small skinless boneless chicken breasts

4 slices of smoked back bacon

8 slices of sourdough bread

1 romaine lettuce heart, leaves separated

1 oz. Parmesan cheese, pared into shavings

sea salt and freshly ground black pepper

olive oil, for brushing

Caesar dressing

¼ cup Mayonnaise (page 52)

4 anchovies in oil, drained and finely chopped

1 garlic clove, crushed

1 teaspoon Worcestershire sauce

1 teaspoon white wine vinegar

½ teaspoon Dijon mustard

Serves 4

chicken steak burger
with caesar dressing

Lay the chicken breast fillets on a chopping board and, using a sharp knife, cut horizontally through the thickest part but don't cut all the way through. Open the breasts out flat. Brush with oil and season with salt and pepper.

Preheat a ridged stovetop grill pan until hot and cook the chicken for 3 to 4 minutes on each side until cooked through. Keep it warm. Cook the bacon on the hot grill pan for 2 to 3 minutes until cooked to your liking. Keep it warm. Toast the sourdough on the grill pan until lightly charred.

Meanwhile, to make the dressing, put the mayonnaise, anchovies, garlic, Worcestershire sauce, vinegar, and mustard in a bowl and beat well. Add salt and pepper to taste.

Spread each slice of sourdough with a little Caesar dressing and top half of them with lettuce, chicken, bacon, and Parmesan shavings. Finish with a second slice of sourdough and serve hot.

1½ lb. skinless boneless chicken breasts, ground

2 garlic cloves, crushed

1 tablespoon chopped fresh rosemary

freshly grated zest and juice of 1 unwaxed lemon

1 egg yolk

⅓ cup dried bread crumbs or matzo meal

1 medium eggplant

2 zucchini

4 slices of focaccia

radicchio or arugula leaves

sea salt and freshly ground black pepper

olive oil, for brushing

Greek Country Salad, to serve (page 56)

Tapenade

⅔ cup black olives, pitted

2 anchovies in oil, drained and rinsed

1 garlic clove, crushed

2 tablespoons capers, rinsed

1 teaspoon Dijon mustard

¼ cup extra virgin olive oil

Serves 4

This open-faced sandwich is full of the flavors of Mediterranean cooking with grilled vegetables, focaccia bread, and salty olive tapenade.

chicken burger
with grilled vegetables

To make the tapenade, put the olives, anchovies, garlic, capers, mustard, and oil in a food processor and blend to form a fairly smooth paste. Season to taste with pepper. Transfer to a dish, cover, and store in the refrigerator for up to 5 days.

Put the chicken, garlic, rosemary, lemon zest and juice, egg yolk, bread crumbs, and some salt and pepper in a food processor and pulse until smooth. Transfer the mixture to a bowl, cover, and chill for 30 minutes. Divide the mixture into 4 portions and shape into patties.

Cut the eggplant into 12 slices and the zucchini into 12 thin strips. Brush with oil and season with salt and pepper. Grill or broil the vegetables for 2 to 3 minutes on each side until charred and softened. Keep them warm.

Meanwhile, brush the chicken patties lightly with oil and grill or broil for 5 minutes on each side until lightly charred and cooked through. Keep them warm.

Toast the focaccia and top each slice with radicchio or arugula leaves, patties, grilled vegetables, and some tapenade. Serve hot with Greek country salad.

The inspiration for this burger comes from a delicious turkey, mustard, and cranberry sandwich I used to order many years ago in a London café. Here, ground turkey is flavored with mustard and the cooked burger is served with a delicious cranberry and onion relish.

1½ lb. skinless turkey breast, coarsely chopped

4 slices of fatty bacon, coarsely chopped

2 tablespoons wholegrain mustard

2 tablespoons chopped fresh flat leaf parsley

½ teaspoon smoked paprika

4 burger buns, cut in half

a handful of watercress

sea salt and freshly ground black pepper

peanut or safflower oil, for sautéing

Cranberry and onion relish

2 tablespoons olive oil

2 red onions, thinly sliced

⅓ cup dried cranberries

1 tablespoon balsamic vinegar

½ cup cranberry sauce

Serves 4

turkey burger
with cranberry and onion relish

To make the cranberry and onion relish, heat the oil in a saucepan, add the onions, and sauté over medium heat for 20 to 25 minutes until caramelized, stirring occasionally.

Meanwhile, soak the cranberries in the vinegar until required. Add to the onions with the cranberry sauce and 2 tablespoons water and cook for 10 minutes until thickened. Season to taste with salt and pepper and set aside to cool.

Put the turkey and bacon in a food processor and process until coarsely ground. Transfer to bowl, add the mustard, parsley, paprika, and some salt and pepper and work together with your hands until evenly mixed. Cover and chill for 30 minutes. Divide into 4 portions and shape into patties.

Heat a shallow layer of peanut or safflower oil in a skillet, add the turkey patties, and sauté for 4 to 5 minutes on each side until cooked through. Keep them warm.

Toast the buns and fill with watercress, patties, and the cranberry and onion relish. Serve hot.

vegetarian

1¼ cups dried chickpeas

1 small onion, finely chopped

2 garlic cloves, crushed

½ bunch of fresh flat-leaf parsley

½ bunch of fresh cilantro

2 teaspoons ground coriander

½ teaspoon baking powder

4 hero rolls

a handful of salad leaves

2 tomatoes, chopped

sea salt and freshly ground black pepper

peanut or safflower oil, for shallow frying

Tahini yogurt sauce

½ cup thick plain yogurt

1 tablespoon tahini paste

1 garlic clove, crushed

½ tablespoon freshly squeezed lemon juice

1 tablespoon extra virgin olive oil

Serves 4

Falafels are Egyptian bean patties traditionally served in pita bread with salad leaves and hummus. Here they make a great burger filling with a tangy yogurt dressing. Tahini is sesame seed paste and is available in supermarkets.

spiced falafel burger

Put the dried chickpeas in a large bowl and add cold water to cover them by at least 5 inches. Let soak overnight. Drain the chickpeas well, transfer to a food processor, and grind them coarsely. Add the onion, garlic, parsley, cilantro, ground coriander, baking powder, and some salt and pepper and blend until very smooth. Transfer to a bowl, cover, and chill for 30 minutes.

To make the tahini sauce, put the yogurt, tahini, garlic, lemon juice, and olive oil in a bowl and whisk until smooth. Season to taste with salt and pepper and set aside until required.

Using wet hands, shape the chickpea mixture into 12 small or 8 medium patties. Heat the oil in a skillet, add the patties, and sauté for 3 minutes on each side until golden and cooked through. Drain on paper towels.

Cut the rolls in half and fill with 2 to 3 patties, tahini yogurt sauce, salad leaves, and chopped tomato. Serve hot.

2 tablespoons olive oil

1 onion, chopped

1 garlic clove, crushed

2 teaspoons ground coriander

1 teaspoon ground cumin

14 oz. canned red kidney beans, drained

8 oz. marinated or smoked tofu

1½ cups fresh whole-wheat bread crumbs

⅓ cup crunchy peanut butter

2 tablespoons chopped fresh cilantro

1 egg, lightly beaten

2 whole-wheat burger buns, cut in half

a few fresh mint, basil, and cilantro leaves

sea salt and freshly ground black pepper

all-purpose flour, for dusting

peanut oil, for shallow frying

sweet chile sauce, to serve

Serves 4

Look for the varieties of tofu that come ready-marinated or smoked to add extra flavor to these burgers. Both are readily available from larger supermarkets and natural food stores.

tofu and bean burger

Heat the olive oil in a skillet, add the onion, garlic, and spices, and sauté gently for 10 minutes until the onion is softened but not browned. Let cool. Transfer the onion mixture to a food processor, add the beans, tofu, bread crumbs, peanut butter, cilantro, egg, salt, and pepper and blend until smooth. Transfer the mixture to a bowl, cover, and chill for 30 minutes.

Using wet hands, divide the mixture into 8 portions and shape into patties. Dust them lightly with flour. Heat a shallow layer of peanut oil in a skillet, add the patties, and sauté for 3 to 4 minutes on each side until crisp and heated through.

Lightly toast the buns and top each half with 2 patties, fresh herbs, and some sweet chile sauce. Serve hot.

½ cup bulgur wheat

1 lb. sweet potatoes, cubed

1½ tablespoons olive oil, plus extra for shallow frying

1 small onion, finely chopped

1 garlic clove, crushed

1 tablespoon curry powder

½ cup blanched almonds, finely chopped

2 tablespoons chopped fresh cilantro

1 egg, lightly beaten

¼ cup chickpea flour or all-purpose flour

4 herbed rolls or chapatti bread

a handful of salad leaves

about 2 inches cucumber, sliced

¼ cup mango chutney

sea salt and freshly ground black pepper

To serve (optional)

lime pickle

plain yogurt

Serves 4

You can either add some lime pickle and natural yogurt to these nutty burgers or serve them rolled in warm chapatti bread. Bulgur is a cracked wheat available from supermarkets and natural food stores.

curried sweet potato burgers

Put the bulgur in a heatproof bowl, add boiling water to cover by 1 inch, and set aside to soak for 20 minutes until the bulgur is tender. Drain well.

Meanwhile, steam the potatoes for 10 to 15 minutes until cooked. Drain well and mash with a potato masher or fork. Heat the oil in a skillet, add the onion, garlic, and curry powder, and sauté for 10 minutes until the onion has softened.

Put the bulgur, mashed potato, onion mixture, almonds, cilantro, egg, flour, and some salt and pepper in a bowl. Work together with your hands until evenly mixed. Cover and chill for 30 minutes. Using wet hands, divide the mixture into 8 portions and shape into patties.

Heat a shallow layer of oil in a skillet, add the patties, and sauté gently for 3 to 4 minutes on each side until golden and heated through. Toast the rolls and fill with the patties, salad leaves, cucumber slices, and mango chutney. Top with some lime pickle and plain yogurt, if using, and serve hot.

Mushrooms, with their meaty texture and earthy flavor, provide vegetarians with a great meat-free alternative to hamburgers. Here they are served with garlic sauce, but you can also serve them more traditionally with mustard, salad, cheese, and pickles.

mushroom burgers
with caramelized garlic aïoli

8 portobello mushrooms

¼–⅓ cup olive oil

4 large burger buns, cut in half

¼ cup Chile Relish (see page 19)

a handful of arugula

sea salt and freshly ground black pepper

Caramelized garlic aïoli

1 large whole head of garlic

2 egg yolks

1 teaspoon Dijon mustard

1 teaspoon freshly squeezed lemon juice

1 cup olive oil

Serves 4

To make the caramelized garlic aïoli, wrap the garlic head in foil and bake in a preheated oven at 400°F for 45 to 50 minutes until the garlic is really soft. Let cool, then squeeze the garlic purée out of each clove into a bowl.

Put the egg yolks, mustard, lemon juice, salt, and the garlic purée in a food processor and blend briefly until frothy. With the motor running, gradually pour in the oil through the funnel until the sauce is thickened and all the oil has been incorporated. Transfer to a bowl, cover the surface with plastic wrap, and chill until required.

Peel the mushroom caps and trim the stalks so they are flat with the caps. Brush lightly with oil, season with salt and pepper, and grill or broil for 4 to 5 minutes on each side until softened and cooked through.

Toast the buns and fill with the mushrooms, caramelized garlic aïoli, chile relish, and some arugula leaves. Serve hot.

The smoky flavor of grilled eggplant and the basil pesto give these burgers a distinctive Mediterranean accent. You could replace the sliced tomatoes with semi-dried ones if you like.

1 large eggplant, about 1½ lb.

¼ cup extra virgin olive oil

1 tablespoon balsamic vinegar

1 garlic clove, crushed

4 soft bread rolls, cut in half

2 beefsteak tomatoes, thickly sliced

8 oz. mozzarella cheese, sliced

a handful of arugula

sea salt and freshly ground black pepper

Pesto

1½ cups fresh basil leaves

1 garlic clove, crushed

¼ cup pine nuts

scant ½ cup extra virgin olive oil

2 tablespoons freshly grated Parmesan cheese

Serves 4

chunky eggplant burgers
with pesto

To make the pesto, put the basil, garlic, pine nuts, oil, and some salt and pepper in a food processor and blend until fairly smooth. Transfer to a bowl, stir in the cheese, and add more salt and pepper to taste. Set aside until required.

Cut the eggplant into ½-inch slices. Put the oil, garlic, vinegar, salt, and pepper in a bowl, whisk to mix, then brush over the eggplant slices. Arrange on a foil-lined broiler pan and broil under a preheated hot broiler for 3 to 4 minutes on each side until well browned and softened.

Lightly toast the rolls and top with a slice of eggplant. Spread with pesto, add another slice of eggplant, then add a slice of tomato and mozzarella. Sprinkle with more pesto, then top with a few arugula leaves. Put the tops on the rolls and serve hot.

on the side ...

It is best to choose evenly sized potatoes for fries so you end up with them roughly the same size. Use an electric deep-fryer or a deep saucepan for frying, and add the uncooked fries to the oil in small batches. If using a saucepan, use a deep-fryer thermometer to check the temperature of the oil.

french fries

2 lb. frying potatoes, such as russets

sea salt

peanut or safflower oil, for deep-frying

an electric deep-fryer (optional)

Serves 4

Cut the potatoes into ½-inch slices, then cut these slices into ½-inch thick sticks. Put them in a bowl of cold water and let soak for 15 minutes. Drain well and dry thoroughly using a clean, dry dish towel.

Pour 2 inches depth of oil into a deep, heavy saucepan. Heat gently until the oil reaches 300°F on a deep-fryer thermometer. Cook the fries, in batches, for 5 to 6 minutes until lightly golden and cooked through. Drain on paper towels and set aside until required.

Increase the heat of the oil to 350°F and cook the fries again, in batches, for 1 to 2 minutes until crisp and golden. Drain on paper towels, transfer to a large bowl, and season lightly with salt. Serve hot.

Variation Shoestring Potatoes

Cut the potatoes into ⅛-inch slices, then again into ⅛-inch thick strips. Wash well under cold running water and dry thoroughly using a clean, dry dish towel. Heat 2 inches depth of oil in a deep, heavy skillet until it reaches 350°F on a deep-fryer thermometer. Add the potato strips and fry, in batches, for 2 to 3 minutes until crisp and golden. Drain on paper towels. Serve hot, sprinkled with salt.

mayonnaise

Homemade mayonnaise has a far nicer flavor and consistency than bought versions and using a food processor makes the job simple.

3 egg yolks

2 teaspoons Dijon mustard

2 teaspoons white wine vinegar or freshly squeezed lemon juice

½ teaspoon sea salt

1¼ cups olive oil

Makes a scant 2 cups

Put the egg yolks, mustard, vinegar or lemon juice, and salt in a food processor and blend briefly until foaming. With the blade running, gradually pour in the oil through the funnel until the sauce is thick and glossy.

If the sauce becomes too thick, add 1 to 2 tablespoons boiling water and blend again. Taste the mayonnaise and add a little more salt if necessary.

Transfer to a bowl and cover the surface with plastic wrap. Refrigerate for up to 3 days, and use as required.

Variations

Mustard Mayonnaise

2 tablespoons wholegrain mustard, such as stoneground

Make the mayonnaise following the method in the main recipe, left, but omitting the Dijon mustard. Transfer to a bowl and stir in the wholegrain mustard. Use as required or store as before.

Herb Mayonnaise

1 recipe Mayonnaise

¾ cup fresh herbs, such as basil, parsley, or tarragon

You can use a single herb or a mixture of herbs to add a lovely fresh flavor to mayonnaise.

Make the mayonnaise following the method in the main recipe, left. Add the herbs to the food processor and blend until the sauce is speckled green. Use as required or store as before.

Aïoli

1 recipe Mayonnaise

2 garlic cloves, crushed

Make the mayonnaise following the method in the main recipe, left, adding the crushed garlic at the same time as the mustard and vinegar. Blend until thickened. Use as required or store as before.

homemade tomato ketchup

Homemade ketchup tastes fantastic. It is simple to make and will store well for up to 5 days or for several weeks in a sterilized jar (page 4). Store in the refrigerator.

2 tablespoons olive oil

1 onion, finely chopped

2 garlic cloves, crushed

one 28-oz. can Italian tomatoes, drained and very finely chopped

½ cup red wine vinegar

¾ cup brown sugar

2 tablespoons molasses

2 tablespoons tomato paste

1 teaspoon Dijon mustard

2 bay leaves

1 teaspoon sea salt

½ teaspoon freshly ground black pepper

Makes about 1¾ cups

Heat the oil in a saucepan, add the onion and garlic, and sauté gently for 10 minutes until softened. Add all the remaining ingredients, bring to a boil, and simmer gently for 30 minutes until thickened and reduced by about one-third. Strain the sauce, let cool, and pour into a clean bottle. Use as required or store in the refrigerator for up to 5 days.

hot and smoky barbecue sauce

Like tomato ketchup, this sauce will keep longer if stored in a sterilized jar (page 4). Pour the sauce into the prepared jar as soon as it is made. Let cool, seal, and refrigerate.

one 14-oz. can Italian tomatoes, drained and very finely chopped

⅓ cup maple syrup

2 tablespoons molasses

2 tablespoons Homemade Tomato Ketchup (see left)

2 tablespoons white wine vinegar

2 tablespoons Worcestershire sauce

1 tablespoon hot chile sauce

2 teaspoons Dijon mustard

1 teaspoon garlic powder

1 teaspoon smoked paprika

sea salt and freshly ground black pepper

Makes 1½ cups

Put all the ingredients in a saucepan, bring to a boil, and simmer gently for 15 minutes until thickened and reduced. Add salt and pepper, then let cool completely. Pour the sauce into a clean jar and store in the refrigerator for up to 5 days. If using sterilized jars, pour the hot sauce directly into the jar. When cold, seal, and store in the refrigerator. It will keep for several weeks.

greek country salad

Try to buy very ripe tomatoes that are still firm but full of flavor.

4 beefsteak tomatoes

1 romaine lettuce heart, sliced

2 small cucumbers, sliced

1¾ cups Kalamata olives, pitted

8 oz. feta cheese, crumbled (optional)

1 teaspoon dried oregano

Dressing

¼ cup extra virgin olive oil

4 teaspoons red wine vinegar

½ teaspoon sugar

sea salt and freshly ground black pepper

Serves 4

Cut the tomatoes into wedges. Put them in a large bowl along with the lettuce, cucumber, olives, and feta, if using.

Put all the dressing ingredients in a bowl, whisk well, then drizzle over the salad and toss well until evenly coated. Sprinkle with the oregano and serve at once.

sour cream coleslaw

You could use plain light, rather than sour cream if you like, although I love the sharp flavor of sour cream.

1 cup shredded white cabbage

1 cup shredded red cabbage

1¼ cups grated carrots

½ white onion, thinly sliced

1 teaspoon sea salt, plus extra for seasoning

2 teaspoons sugar

1 tablespoon white wine vinegar

¼ cup Mayonnaise (page 52)

¼ cup sour cream

freshly ground black pepper

Makes 1 lb.

Put the white and red cabbage, carrots, and onion in a colander and sprinkle with the salt, sugar, and vinegar. Stir well and let drain over a bowl for 20 minutes.

Transfer the vegetables to a clean dish towel and squeeze out any excess liquid. Put them in a large bowl and stir in the mayonnaise and cream. Season to taste with salt and pepper and serve.

arugula, radicchio, and crisp bacon salad

You can use just arugula if you like—just increase to 3 bundles.

6 slices of bacon

1 garlic clove, peeled but left whole

2 bundles of large arugula leaves

1 radicchio, torn into bite-size pieces

½ cup pine nuts, toasted in a dry skillet

Dressing

3 tablespoons extra virgin olive oil

1 tablespoon freshly squeezed lemon juice

sea salt and freshly ground black pepper

Serves 4

Heat a skillet until hot, add the bacon, and sauté for 2 to 3 minutes on each side until golden. Let cool and break into small pieces. Rub the inside of a large salad bowl with the garlic clove. Wash and spin the arugula and radicchio leaves. Transfer to the bowl, and add the bacon pieces and pine nuts.

Put all the dressing ingredients in a small bowl, whisk well, then sprinkle it over the salad. Toss gently to coat the leaves evenly and serve at once.

romaine heart salad with creamy herb dressing

You can vary the flavor of this dressing by using different herbs, such as chives or mint.

4 baby romaine lettuce hearts

Dressing

¼ cup extra virgin olive oil

2 tablespoons sour cream

1 tablespoon white wine vinegar

¼ teaspoon sugar

2 scallions, finely chopped

1 tablespoon finely chopped fresh herbs, such as tarragon, basil, and parsley

sea salt and freshly ground black pepper

Serves 4

Separate the lettuce leaves. Wash them, dry them in a salad spinner or on paper towels, and put them on a large platter. Put all the dressing ingredients in a small bowl and whisk until smooth. Season to taste with salt and pepper. Sprinkle the dressing over the lettuce, toss gently to coat the leaves evenly, and serve at once.

smoothies and shakes

triple berry smoothie

When fresh berries are out of season, you can use frozen fruits to make this smoothie. Thaw the frozen berries at room temperature before blending.

8 oz. strawberries, hulled

8 oz. raspberries

8 oz. blueberries or blackberries

⅔ cup cranberry juice

8 oz. frozen strawberry yogurt

Serves 4

Put all the ingredients in a blender and purée until smooth. Pour into 4 glasses and serve at once.

tropical fruit smoothie

The best time to make a smoothie is when you can get really good quality fruit in season. Vary the fruit according to availability—try melon, peaches, apricots, or papaya.

8 oz. peeled mango

8 oz. peeled pineapple

2 bananas, peeled and chopped

⅔ cup tropical fruit juice

½ cup plain yogurt

a handful of ice cubes

Serves 4

Put all the ingredients in a blender and purée until smooth. Pour into 4 glasses and serve at once.